1 Abbot Islip Towers
2 West Door
3 Builders' Wheel
4 S.W. Tower Unfinished
5 Nave   (Dollar
6 Central Lantern (Islip)
7 N. Transept. Royal
    Entrance to Abbey
8 St. Margaret's Church
9 Sanctuary
10 Henry VII's Lady Chapel
11 Royal Private Entrance
12 Cemetery

13 Abbot's Lodging
14 Jerusalem Chamber
15 Jericho Parlour
16 Hall
17 Kitchen
18 Apartments
19 Gallery
20 Cloister Entrance
21 Parlour
22 Cloister
23 Night Stairs
24 Vestry
25 Chapel of St. Faith
26 Entrance to
27 Chapter House

28 Library
29 Chapel of St. Dunstan
30 Monk's Dormitory
31 Bell Tower
32 Rere-dorter
33 Farmery Cloister former-
    -ly Nave of
34 Chapel of St. Katherine
35 Farmerer's Hall
36 Infirmary Garden
37 Fish Ponds
38 Cellarer's Building lay
    Dormitory over
39 Blackstole Tower
40 Prior's Lodging
41 Entrance to
42 Dark Cloister
43 Frater
44 Kitchen
45 Misericorde

46 Grammar School
47 Water Conduit
48 Entrance to Bayliff's
49 Hospice
50 Stables
51 South Gateway
52 Broad Sanctuary
53 Little Sanctuary
54 Bell Tower
55 Great Sanctuary
56 Abbey Wall
57 Abbey Gate House
58 Jail
59 Abbey Court Gate
60 Bishop of London's Prison
61 The Elms (Dean's Yard)
62 King's Alms Houses
    (Henry VII Little Almoury
63 Poor Men's Lodging
64 Great Almonry (Lady
    Margaret)
65 River Tyburn
66 Long Ditch (west)
67 Orchard, 67a Tot Hill-
68 Bakehouse   (-Fields
69 Abbey Farm
70 Abbey Mill
71 Garden Wall
72 Long Ditch (south)
73 Abbot's Mill tidal wheel
74 Abbot's Garden
75 Abbey Kitchen Garden

A To Charing Cross
B Long Ditch (north) the
    "Clowson"
C King Street
D Theeving Lane
E High Tower, West
    Gateway
F St. Stephen's Alley Canonry

G Gateway to Canon's Row
H Palace Court
I Woolstaple
J Clock Tower
K Weyhouse
L Westminster Stairs
M Fountain
N Duchy of Lancaster

O South Gate
P Westminster Hall
Q Star Chamber
R Our Lady of the Pew
S Cloister
T St. Stephen's
U St. Stephen's
V The White Hall

W Painted Chamber
X Westminster Palace
    Boat house & Stairs
Y Jewel Tower (Z)

D1157052

To Gram,

These pictures are only half as impressive as actually seeing Westminister but I hope you can enjoy its beauty in some small way.

Love,

Pat

The Glory of Westminster Abbey

TEXT BY DAVID CARPENTER
PUBLISHED BY JARROLD & SONS LIMITED, NORWICH
FOR THE DEAN AND CHAPTER OF WESTMINSTER

Contents

	Page
The Origins of Westminster Abbey	3
The Church of King Henry III	4
The Completion of the Nave	4
Saint Edward the Confessor's Chapel	5
King Henry VII's Chapel	6
The Reformation and the Abbey's Later History	7
The Abbey Today	8
Illustrations	9–48

All photographs are copyright Jarrold & Sons Ltd, Norwich, except for those on

page 25 (Offa's Charter), page 28 (both pictures), page 29 (Combat scene), page 34 (Eltham weepers), page 39 (Henry V Sculpture), page 40 (Henry VII Chapel), page 41 (both pictures), which are the copyright of the Dean and Chapter of Westminster;

the plate on page 32 (Islip Roll) which appears by permission of John R. Freeman & Co. and is an ultra-violet photograph;

the plate on page 37 (Richard II portrait) which appears by permission of the National Gallery.

The Jarrold pictures were taken by Richard H. Tilbrook and the Westminster Abbey pictures by the late R. P. Howgrave Graham, F.S.A., Assistant Keeper of the Muniments. The reconstructional drawings on pages 26 and 46 are by the late Arthur Henderson, F.S.A.; the second being the product of lengthy research with the present Librarian of Westminster Abbey, Lawrence E. Tanner, C.V.O., F.S.A.

Printed and bound in Great Britain by Jarrold & Sons Ltd, Norwich.   853 06521 7

The Origins of Westminster Abbey

The Collegiate Church of St Peter in Westminster, to give Westminster Abbey its official title, has many different legends concerning its earliest origins. Perhaps the most engaging tells of a church being built on the island of Thorney in the middle of the Thames by Sebert, King of the East Saxons. As it nears completion St Peter miraculously appears and is ferried across to the island by some fishermen who are struck with terror as they see the whole building fill with light. The Saint tells them that he has consecrated the church; a wonderful draught of salmon will reward them for their services but they must not fish again on Sunday!

It is probably true that the Abbey once stood on an island formed by the Thames—as is sometimes thought to be shown by the oyster-shells still dug up in the garden within the precincts—but the first known reference to the church is in a bare grant of land from Algeric, Bishop of Dorchester, in 693. The name first appears in another grant from Offa, King of the Mercians, to the monastery 'in that terrible place Westmunster' (c. 785). However, in medieval times, the earlier legends were so strong that in 1308 a tomb, which can still be seen and is said to contain Sebert's remains, was set up in the south ambulatory of the present church.

Nonetheless the name most generally associated with the foundation of the Abbey is, of course, that of King Edward the Confessor (1042–66). He built an entirely new church which he just lived to see consecrated on Holy Innocents' Day 1065 and in which he was buried. It was to this new church that William the Conqueror came to be crowned on Christmas Day 1066, thereby setting a precedent followed by every succeeding King and Queen of England, except Edward V (the elder of the Princes in the Tower) and Edward VIII.

Nothing remains today of the magnificent church of the Confessor save only a few piers discovered beneath the floor of the present high altar. As the Abbey, however, was a monastery a great many buildings were necessary for the housing and general welfare of the monks. Some of these do survive, notably the long vaulted Undercroft (1066–1100) which formed the ground floor of the Dormitory. Its northern end, the Pyx Chamber, used to house the King's treasury for the King, with his royal palace of Westminster adjoining the church, looked upon the Abbey very much as his personal possession. In 1303, however, there was a great robbery and the Abbot of Westminster and his forty-eight monks, owing to a 'wicked suspicion', were imprisoned for a time in the Tower of London. A fragment of human skin, which still lines one of the doors leading into the treasury, perhaps indicates the severity of the punishment the robbers suffered. In the south walk of the present cloister may be seen the much-worn marble effigies of three of the earliest Abbots. The centre one is that of Gilbert Crispin (1085–1117), a friend of Lanfranc, and probably the most learned and holy of all.

The Church of King Henry III

One of Henry III's (1216–72) great passions was his devotion to Edward the Confessor who had been made a saint in 1161. He therefore desired to rehouse the Confessor's body in a magnificently contemporary building. The eastern part of the old church was pulled down in July 1245 and the King, straining his finances to the limit, pushed the work forward with great haste. On 13 October 1269 this new church was consecrated and the Confessor's body was placed in a new shrine behind the present high altar where it remains to this day. The Abbey was then completed as far west as the present choir screen and thus the apse, transepts and choir, as we now see them, are all the work of Henry III.

The church, as it presented itself to Henry on that day, must have been one of the most sumptuous buildings in the whole of the Gothic world. It showed extensive French influence, in the form of windows, modelled almost exactly on those at Rheims; in the constructional system of the vault and flying buttresses; and particularly in its great height. (At 103 feet to the crown of the vault it is the tallest medieval building in Britain.) Yet, for all this, the Abbey was still overpoweringly insular and to quote Sir Gilbert Scott 'a great French thought expressed in excellent English'. Indeed, though the name of the inspired mason who conceived the design was Henry de Reynes, which has led to the suggestion that he came from Rheims, there can be little doubt, in fact, that he was an Englishman. The Abbey's most noticeable characteristic, its decorative elaboration, had been developing in England for many years. After Westminster had fully explored its possibilities, it was in part to form the basis of the decorated style of architecture, as for instance at Exeter and in the Angel Choir at Lincoln. At Westminster there was hardly a single portion of plain wall surface. Round the whole length of the church, at ground-level, a wall arcade ran which, especially in the eastern chapels, was almost overburdened with sculpture and in the choir had a magnificent series of heraldic shields. The spandrels of the great arcades were filled with diaper which was then probably painted gilt on a red background; the triforium was elaborately moulded and adorned with stiff leaf foliage; the piers were highly polished marble; the bosses of the vault were gilded; the figure sculpture, noticeably the angels in the transepts, were picked out in the colours of life and the few areas of plain stone were almost certainly filled with painting.

The glass was designed with reference to this many coloured interior. It was mostly grisaille (that is plain with a silver tint) to let in as much light as possible and in it were set heraldic shields and medallions portraying biblical scenes. The final impression must have been one of dazzling richness and splendour.

The Completion of the Nave

The Abbey stood in this unfinished condition—completed as far west as the present choir screen—for over 100 years, until 1376 when Abbot Litlington (1362–86), using the fortune left to the monastery by his predecessor Cardinal Simon Langham, began the finishing of the nave. Despite help from kings Richard II (1377–99), Henry V (1413–22) and Edward IV

(1461–83) the work took over 150 years; it was not finally completed until the time of the great Abbot Islip (1500–32) and even then no western towers had been built.

The nave itself is almost unique, for apart from changes in mouldings and the cessation of the diaper work, it was completed, despite the lapse of years, in the same style as that of Henry III. The great master mason 'original enough not to seek after originality in his work' was almost certainly Henry Yevele and it was his realization that the thirteenth-century design was one he could not better that gives the nave 'a unity and harmony which largely contribute to its special beauty'.

Saint Edward the Confessor's Chapel

In 1269 the shrine of the Confessor stood alone behind the high altar. Like the floor of red and green porphyry, glass mosaic and purbeck marble on which it stands, the shrine is the work of the famous Roman Cosmati school and is signed by Peter the Roman. It was richly decorated with jewels and mosaic and while much of this disappeared at the Reformation, the shrine still survives, though reconstructed. It is alone among important surviving shrines in Britain in still containing the body of its saint. The coffin was revealed during preparations for the coronation of James II (1685) when a hole was somehow made in it. One John Taylour records: 'I drew the head to the hole and view'd it, being very sound and firm, with the upper and nether jaws full of teeth. . . . There was also in the coffin white linen, and gold colour'd flower'd silk, that look't indifferent fresh, but the least stress put thereto shew'd it was well nigh perish't.'

By 1432 this single tomb was surrounded by those of the Kings and Queens of England, who naturally wished to lie near their saintly predecessor. The first additions were the tombs of Henry III (*ob.* 1272) and his daughter-in-law Eleanor of Castile (*ob.* 1290), whose gilt bronze effigies were constructed in 1291 by William Torel. Technically perfect, these are idealizations rather than accurate portraits. The face of Henry is majestic and full of concern, that of Eleanor of consummate grace.

There could hardly be a more striking contrast to these stately monuments than the next addition to the Westminster mausoleum, that of Edward I (1272–1307). It was Edward who had brought back from his Scottish wars the Stone of Scone on which, legend has it, Jacob slept and which had certainly been used for coronations of Kings of Scotland. To contain it, the Coronation Chair was made and the Chair and the Stone (which have always been kept in the Confessor's Chapel) have been used at every coronation since that of Edward II (1307) and have thus, through the centuries, played a unique part in English history. But Edward I's tomb is of plain purbeck marble with no effigy or decoration. An explanation for this may lie in the famous pact that the King made with his son, that his flesh should be boiled, that his heart be sent to the Holy Land and his bones carried at the head of the English army till Scotland was finally subdued. Perhaps the intention was to allow easy access to the body to enable these wishes to be carried out and for this purpose the tomb was left bare.

The next two kings to surround the shrine of the Confessor, Edward III (1327–77) and Richard II (1377–99), have similar tombs and their gilt bronze effigies mark a departure in that there is obviously an attempt at portraiture. The face of Edward III, despite the stylization of hair and beard, is quite clearly modelled on his death mask which survives in the Abbey museum. It is very strong and firm and the weepers, which remain on the ambulatory side of the tomb, fit in with its mood, being calm and without hint of emotion. The effigy of Richard II was made in his lifetime and the face shows striking similarity to the contemporary portrait which may be seen at the west end of the church.

Henry IV (1399–1413), not surprisingly, in view of his deposition of Richard, chose to be buried at Canterbury but his son, Henry V (1413–22), had always shown a love of the Abbey and he determined to be buried there. There was, however, no longer any room in the Confessor's chapel and so it was decided to build an addition on to its eastern end. This, the chantry chapel of Henry V, was, perhaps, constructed intentionally in the form of an 'H' and it is rich in sculpture which depicts him at his coronation and on horseback in full armour. The effigy itself was covered in silver plate and had a solid silver head, but these were stolen at the Reformation and only the bare wooden core remains. Above the chapel on a wooden beam rest the saddle, shield and helmet which were carried at Henry's funeral. A sword which may have belonged to him is preserved in the Abbey library.

In the middle years of the fifteenth century the screen which forms the backing to the High Altar was built, making the Confessor's chapel a separate entity. No further kings were to be buried there, though the pathetic intention of Henry VI (1422–61), to lie by his father, Henry V, is still manifested in the coarsely drawn circuit in the chapel pavement which he caused to be drawn to mark his intended grave.

With its crowded historical associations, the Chapel of the Confessor, a place of pilgrimage in the Middle Ages and the spiritual centre of the Abbey today, takes us back, more than anywhere else in England, to the atmosphere of the medieval world, making us remember the struggles of dead kings and helping us to understand a little the minds and ideals of those who constructed their tombs.

King Henry VII's Chapel

As we walk from the ambulatory up the steep steps into Henry VII's Chapel, such is the contrast in styles between the early English of Henry III and the late Perpendicular of Henry VII (1485–1509), that the effect is of entering an entirely new church. And in view of the new era of English history which is sometimes said to have opened with the reign of Henry it is perhaps fitting that this should be so.

The chapel, begun in 1503 on the site of the old Lady chapel and described by Wren as a 'nice embroidered work' and by John Leland as 'the wonder of the world', is in a way the symbol of the new Tudor monarchy noted for its visible emphasis on the power and elevated position of the King. High up, in the panels of the great fan vaulting, below in the bronze gates and in the frieze of angels, are repeated again and again the Tudor badges of rose and portcullis interspersed with fleurs-de-lis and heraldic beasts. Looking down, as it were with approval, at this manifestation of regal opulence, is the most complete series of sculptured saints in Europe, vigorously, sometimes brilliantly, executed and nearly all in a state of perfect preservation.

The chapel itself shows no sign of Renaissance influence but the tomb of Henry VII, with the masterly effigies of himself and his wife, are by the Italian Torrigiani, who, it is said, had to live outside Italy because of the wrath he had incurred from breaking Michelangelo's nose. The fine effigy of Henry's mother, Lady Margaret Beaufort, in the south aisle of the chapel is also by him.

All the Tudors, except Henry VIII, lie within this chapel. Edward VI (1547–53) is in an unmarked grave under the altar, while Elizabeth has a stately monument in the north aisle with an effigy which is one of the best representations of her in old age. Her coffin stands on that of her half-sister Mary's (1553–8), and the inscription on the monument translates: 'Consorts both in throne and grave, here sleep the two sisters, Elizabeth and Mary, in the hope of one resurrection.' By an ironic twist of fate, under a very similar monument in the opposite aisle, lies Mary Queen of Scots, whom Elizabeth had had executed in 1587. Mary's son, James I (1603–25), brought her body from Peterborough for burial in the Abbey in 1612.

Strangely, perhaps, these mark the last series of royal monuments within the Abbey. James I, Charles II (1660–85), Mary II (1689–94), William III (1689–1702), Anne (1702–14), and George II (1727–60) are all buried in Henry VII's Chapel but they have only inscriptions in the pavement to mark where they lie. There is, however, a small sarcophagus in the north aisle containing the bones of two small boys which were found under a staircase in the Tower of London in 1674 and which may be the bones of the Princes in the Tower, Edward V (1483) and Richard, Duke of York. The child-bride of Richard, Anne Mowbray, whose body was discovered in 1964 on a Stepney building site, has since been reinterred in the chapel. She had probably been removed when the old Lady Chapel was pulled down to make way for Henry's new and splendid masterpiece.

The Reformation and the Abbey's Later History

While the interior of the Abbey was finished by 1528 it was a long time before the exterior was completed by the addition of the western towers, for the Reformation brought an abrupt end to building as may be seen from the uncarved blocks of stone in the wall arcades of the chapels under the towers. Yet the break in continuity at the Reformation was less great than might have been expected for, though the monastery was dissolved and the Abbey became a cathedral church (1540), the Abbot simply became the Dean and some of the monks stayed on as Prebends and Minor Canons. With the reign of Mary (1553–8) and the restoration of the old religion, Westminster was almost alone in being refounded as a monastery. The Abbot at the time was the distinguished preacher John Feckenham, whose most lasting work was to reconstruct the shrine of the Confessor which had been partially destroyed in 1540. On the accession of Elizabeth however (1558) the monastery was again dissolved. Westminster's last monk, Fra Buckley, was to live on till 1610. Elizabeth did not refound the cathedral of her father but instead she established a Dean and twelve Prebendaries who were to constitute the governing body of the Collegiate Church of St Peter, Westminster. The foundation inherited 'all ancient privileges' and this accounts for the position of the Abbey today, for just as the Abbot and Convent had been subject only to the Pope and not to the local bishop or archbishop, so now the Abbey is a 'royal peculiar', subject only to the Queen. Even the Archbishop of Canterbury officiates here, as in the service for Consecration of Bishops, only by leave of the Dean.

While the Abbey's constitution has remained substantially unchanged from 1559 to this day, the fabric has both suffered and gained much. Many of the later monuments have disfigured the beautiful wall arcade, and the whole of the north porch, which was formerly always the royal entrance to the church, has been lost in its original form in the restoration of the early eighteenth and the wholesale reconstruction of the late nineteenth century. The loss has been described as 'probably the most serious single disaster that English sculpture has suffered'. On the other hand the Western towers, designed by Hawksmoor, and built between 1732 and 1745, now provide the most famous view of the Abbey which is known throughout the world. Moreover, that the Abbey stands at all is due in great measure to the successful work of preservation and repair carried out down the centuries, in particular by Sir Christopher Wren and by Sir Gilbert Scott whose efforts preserve the church for us today and for future generations.

The Abbey Today

The Abbey today is, perhaps, more than any other church, the church of the nation and Commonwealth. In it are held great national services from coronations and royal weddings to services in times of national peril such as at the evacuation of Dunkirk. The sovereign attends the service of the Order of the Bath held in Henry VII's Chapel and Westminster is also one of the homes for the distribution of the Royal Maundy. The Abbey too has memorials to so much of our national history. Not only is it, as we have seen, the burial place of kings, but in the South Transept, in and around Poets' Corner, are the graves and monuments of most of our great men of letters, while in the North Transept the statesmen and in the Nave the soldiers, sailors and scientists are gathered. At the west end of the nave is the grave of the Unknown Warrior commemorating the dead of the Great War, while Britain's 'finest hour' is remembered in the Battle of Britain window in the R.A.F. Chapel at the east end of Henry VII's Chapel.

Moreover, with the money from the world-wide appeal, launched by Sir Winston Churchill, in 1953, now himself commemorated in a carved stone at the west end of the Nave, the interior of the church has been thoroughly cleaned and the beautiful whiteness of the stone, so long hidden by layers of London grime, has been revealed. Much too of the Abbey's former colour has been sympathetically restored. The bosses and ribs of the vault are now regilded, the marble piers have been repolished, the choir screen and many of the sixteenth- and seventeenth-century monuments have been repainted in brilliant colours. The Abbey today gives a better idea of the sumptuous building that Henry III beheld on the day of its reconsecration in 1269 than it has done for centuries and its history is correspondingly longer and infinitely richer.

In this view looking east from the Nave the recently polished marble piers and gilded ribs and bosses of the vault show up well. The choir screen marks the division between the work of Henry III (1245–69) and that begun in 1376.

[*Above*] The North Transept (*c.* 1255), sometimes known as the Statesmen's Transept, contains monuments to Chatham, Peel, Disraeli
and Gladstone. In the Middle Ages it formed
the main entrance to the Church.

[*Opposite*] The nave (1376–1528), is almost
unique in preserving the same style as the
earlier part of the building. The glass in the
west window, designed by Joshua Price, was
put up in the reign of George II.

[*Above*] This close-up of the triforium and rose window of the North Transept shows the Censing Angels and the elaborate foliage carving. The glass was designed by Sir James Thornhill in 1721.

[*Opposite*] In the South Transept (*c.* 1255) is seen the effect of the contrasting stone in the vault. Beneath the rose window, restored in the nineteenth century, are seen the famous Censing Angels.

[*Above*] The shrine of St Edward the Confessor was made by the Roman Cosmati family (*c.* 1269) and was once richly decorated with jewels and mosaic. The wooden feretory at the top, newly restored, is sixteenth century.

(*Opposite*) The Presbytery and Apse were the earliest parts completed by Henry III. The present High Altar and Reredos were erected in the nineteenth century to the design of Sir Gilbert Scott and the mosaic of the Last Supper is by Salviati.

The gilt bronze effigy of Eleanor of Castile, wife of Edward I, was constructed by William Torel in 1291 and the iron grille in the background by Master Walter of Durham.

The Coronation Chair was built to the orders
of Edward I in 1300 to hold the Stone of Scone.
Since then it has been used at the Coronation of
every King and Queen of England.

[*Opposite*] The present highly painted choir Screen was built by the then Abbey Surveyor, Edward Blore, in 1828, after the original thirteenth-century work had been unfortunately destroyed.

[*Above*] The grave of the Unknown Warrior at the West End of the Nave is covered by a slab of black Belgian marble from a quarry near Namur. Part of the inscription reads: 'They buried him among the Kings because he had done good toward God and toward his House.'

These two views of Henry VII's Chapel looking
east [*opposite*] and west [*below*] show well the
unique fan vaulting, completed about 1518.
The banners are those of the Knights Grand
Cross of the Bath.

[*Above*] The attractive Cherubs from the tomb of Henry VII are by Torrigiani (*c.* 1509).

[*Opposite*] The altar of Henry VII's Chapel was designed by Sir Walter Tapper in 1935 as a replica of the original destroyed in the Civil War. Under it Edward VI is buried. The picture of the Virgin and Child is by the Italian Bartolomeo Vivarini (late fifteenth century).

[*Left*] This window which commemorates the Battle of Britain was designed by Hugh Easton and is at the east end of Henry VII's Chapel in the Battle of Britain Chapel. It contains the badges of the sixty-three squadrons that took part.

[*Right*] This is the Charter from Offa, King of the Mercians, granting the Abbey some land at Aldenham. It is the earliest Charter the Abbey possesses (*c.* 785) and the name Westminster appears in it for the first time.

[*Below*] The Undercroft is one of the few surviving parts of the Abbey dating back to the Confessor. In medieval times it was used as a general common room by the monks. It now forms the Abbey Museum.

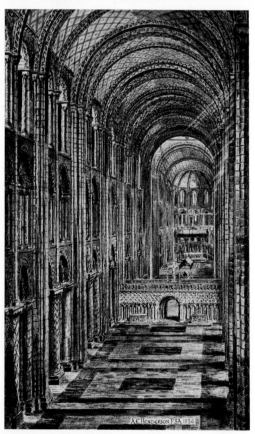

[*Above*] Placed in the South Ambulatory of the present Abbey in 1308, this tomb is supposed to contain the body of King Sebert, the legendary first founder of the Abbey.

[*Left*] This drawing shows what the interior of the Confessor's Church may have been like. Its nave remained in place till 1376.

[*Above right*] The worn marble effigy in the South Cloister is of Abbot Gilbert Crispin (1085–1117). He was the most saintly of all the Abbots.

[*Right*] The tomb of Henry III was made by the Roman Cosmati family (*c.* 1272) and the King's effigy by William Torel in 1291. The three niches were to house relics and the small cavity in the column behind Henry's head is said to have held a phial of Holy Blood.

[*Left*] This stone head, high up in the North Transept (*c.* 1255), may be intended to represent Henry de Reynes, the Abbey's chief architect.

[*Below*] The four Censing Angels in the Abbey have been described as 'the supreme examples of English medieval art'. The one on the eastern side of the South Transept is here illustrated.

[*Above*] A fine view looking up at the extreme
east end of the Apse. This was the earliest part
finished by Henry III in his rebuilding (*c.* 1245).

Combat scenes are particularly common in the
thirteenth-century sculpture in the Abbey. This
one of a centaur fighting a dragon is in the
Muniment Room above the East Cloister.

[*Below*] This painting of St Peter is part of the
original thirteenth-century Retable or Altar
Piece which for years lay unrecognised as part
of a wax work case. It is now in the South
Ambulatory.

[*Above*] These large wall paintings (*c.* 1280–1300), in the South Transept represent the incredulity of St Thomas [*left*] and St Christopher.

[*Above*] The wall arcade in St Benedict's Chapel has been restored to its original brilliance. The monument is to Gabriel Goodman, second Dean of Westminster (1561–1601).

[*Above*] This print from an engraving by W. Hollar shows the Abbey as it was left by Abbot Islip before the addition of the western towers.

[*Below*] The tomb of Cardinal Simon Langham, Abbot of Westminster (1349–62), is in St Benedict's Chapel. It was his vast fortune which enabled work to begin on the completion of the nave.

[*Left*] This pen-and-ink drawing of the funeral of Abbot Islip (1532) is the only representation of the interior of the Abbey before the Reformation. The rood seen here over the high altar has entirely disappeared.

[*Above right*] Consisting of an eye and a boy falling from a tree (a slip) this little sculptured scene from Islip's Chantry Chapel puns on his name.

[*Below right*] These tombs with their almost unique canopies are to Edmund Crouchback (*d.* 1296), brother of Edward I, and to Aymer de Valence (*d.* 1324), Edward's cousin.

[*Above*] The canopy of the Crouchback tomb contains this equestrian portrait of him.

[*Above*] Two of the weepers from the Crouchback tomb.

[*Above*] These dramatic weepers are on the tomb of John of Eltham (*ob.* 1337), murdered by his brother Edward III.

[*Below*] John of Eltham's alabaster effigy is one of the finest in the Abbey and was probably executed by the same artist as that of Edward II at Gloucester.

[*Left*] The tomb of Edward III (1327–77), seen from the ambulatory, was designed by Henry Yevele. The weepers are of Edward's children, the one in the left corner being the Black Prince.

[*Below left*] Edward's gilt bronze effigy was made by John Orchard who was also responsible for the Black Prince's at Canterbury.

[*Below*] The tomb of Richard II and his beloved wife Anne of Bohemia dates from 1394 to 1395 and was also designed by Yevele. The effigies are by Nicholas Broker and Godfrey Prest.

[*Above*] This contemporary portrait of Richard II, a great benefactor to the Abbey, is at the west end of the Nave.

[*Below*] The chantry chapel of Henry V begun
in 1438 was perhaps constructed intentionally
in the form of an 'H'. The tomb lies behind the
grating though the effigy has lost all its silver
fittings.

[*Above*] This view from the upper storey of the Chapel shows the saddle, helmet and shield which were carried at Henry's funeral, and beyond is seen the thirteenth century vaulting of the Apse.

[*Right*] This dashing equestrian portrait of Henry is one of the many sculptures which adorn the Chapel.

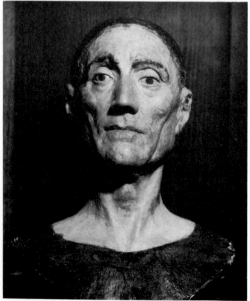

[*Above*] Part of the series of saints which run round Henry VII's Chapel at triforium level and the frieze of angels with portcullis, rose and fleurs-de-lis beneath.

[*Left*] The death mask of Henry VII (*ob.* 1509) is now in the Museum. It formed part of a whole effigy of him carried at his funeral.

[*Right*] The iron grille surrounding Henry VII's tomb contains a number of small statuettes. This one is of St George and the Dragon.

[*Below*] The grill seen here in full, though not begun till 1508, shows no sign of classical influence.

[*Right*] The tomb of Queen Elizabeth (*ob.* 1603), in the north aisle of Henry VII Chapel, was constructed in 1606 by Maximilian Colt.

[*Left*] The tomb of Henry VII itself is by the Italian Torrigiani. This medallion on the south side is of St Edward the Confessor and St Vincent.

[*Below*] Torrigiani was also responsible for the effigy of Henry VII's mother, Lady Margaret Beaufort, which is in the south aisle of the chapel.

MEMORIÆ ÆTERNÆ

ELIZABETHÆ ANGLIÆ FRANCIÆ ET HIBERNIÆ
REGINÆ R HENRICI VIII FILIÆ R HEN VII NEPTI R
ED IIII PRONEPTI PATRIÆ PARENTI RELIGIONIS
ET BONARVM ARTIVM ALTRICI PLVRIMARVM
LINGVARVM PERITIA PRÆCLARIS TVM ANIMI
TVM CORPORIS DOTIBVS REGINÆQ VIRTVTIBVS
SVPRA SEXVM PRINCIPI
INCOMPARABILI
IACOBVS MAGNÆ BRITANNIÆ FRANCIÆ ET
HIBERNIÆ REX VIRTVTVM ET REGNORVM
HÆRES BENE MERENTI PIE
POSVIT

REGNO CONSORES
& VRNA HIC OBDOR
MIMVS ELIZABETHA

ET MARIA SORORES
IN SPE RESVRREC=
TIONIS

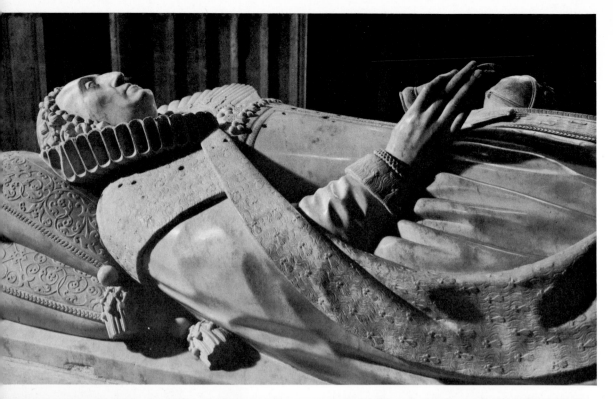

[*Above*] This humorous scene is from one of the early sixteenth-century Misericords in the Chapel. It is a theme often found in Medieval wood carvings.

[*Top left*] The effigy of Queen Elizabeth is one of the best representations of her in old age.

[*Bottom left*] The effigy of Mary Queen of Scots, in the South aisle of Henry VII Chapel, is some years later in date than that of Elizabeth and is by Cornelius Cure.

[*Left*] The cloisters, today very badly decayed, are where the monks spent most of their day.

[*Below*] This reconstruction of the Abbey and its precincts gives some idea of what they may have looked like before the Reformation. Note the builders wheel on the unfinished towers and the fact that the precincts are still surrounded by water.

[*Right*] Chaucer was originally buried in the Abbey because he lived in the precincts. The tomb recognising his fame as a poet was erected in 1558, over 150 years after his death.

[*Below right*] Around Chaucer's tomb in the South Transept are monuments to most of our great men of letters. The central one here is, of course, Shakespeare; the seated figure is Wordsworth.

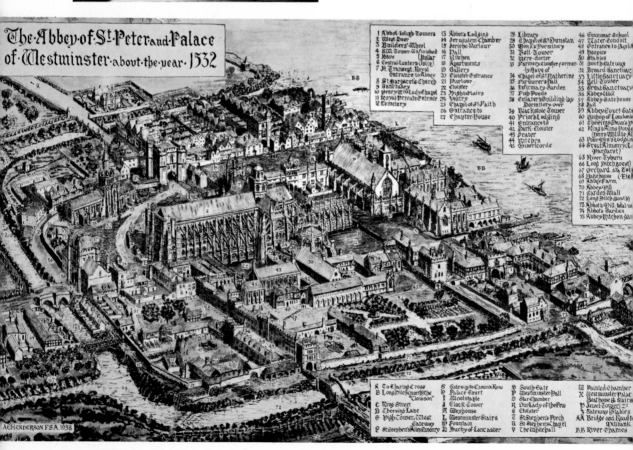

The Abbey of St. Peter and Palace of Westminster about the year 1532

1 Abbot Islyps Towers
2 West Door
3 Builders' Wheel
4 N.W. Tower Unfinished
5 Nave
6 Central Lantern (Islip)
7 N. Transept. Royal Entrance to Abbey
8 St Margarets Church
9 Sanctuary
10 Henry VII Lady Chapel
11 Royal Private Entrance
12 Cemetery
13 Abbot's Lodging
14 Jerusalem Chamber
15 Jericho Parlour
16 Hall
17 Kitchen
18 Apartments
19 Gallery
20 Cloister Entrance
21 Parlour
22 Cloister
23 Night Stairs
24 Vestry
25 Chapel of St Faith
26 Entrance to
27 Chapter House
28 Library
29 Chapel of St Dunstan
30 Monk's Dormitory
31 Rere-dorter
32 Pyx Chamber
33 Farmery & Cloister former-ly Nave of
34 Chapel of St Katherine
35 Farmerer's Hall
36 Infirmary Garden
37 Fish Ponds
38 Cellarer's Building: lay Dormitory over
39 Blackstole Tower
40 Prior's Lodging
41 Entrance to
42 Dark Cloister
43 Frater
44 Kitchen
45 Misericorde
46 Grammar School
47 Water Conduit
48 Entrance to Baylid
49 Hospice
50 Stables
51 South Gate way
52 Broad Sanctuary
53 Little Sanctuary
54 Bell Tower
55 Great Sanctuary
56 Abbey Wall
57 Abbey Gatehouse
58 Jail
59 Abbey Court Gate
60 Bishop of Londons
61 The Fins Deans y
62 King's Alms House (Henry VII Ellie Al
63 Poor Mens Lodging
64 Great Almonry (L Margaret)
65 River Tyburn
66 Long Ditch (West)
67 Orchard 67a Tot
68 Bakehouse (Ele
69 Abbey Farm
70 Abbey Mill
71 Garden Wall
72 Long Ditch (South)
73 Abbot's Mill Mal u
74 Abbot's Garden
75 Abbey Kitchen Ga

A To Charing Cross
B Long Ditch (north the Clowson"
C King Street
D Theeving Lane
E High Tower, West Gateway
F St Stephen's Alley Amonry
G Gateway & Canon's Row
H Palace Court
I Woolstaple
J Clock Tower
K Weyhouse
L Westminster Stairs
M Fountain
N Duchy of Lancaster
O South Gate
P Westminster Hall
Q Star Chamber
R Our Lady of the Pew
S Cloister
T St Stephen's Porch
U St Stephen's Chapel
V The White Hall
W Painted Chamber
X Westminster Palac
Y Boat house & Stairs
Z Jewel Tower 71
P Gateway Stables
AA Bridge and Road to Millbank
BB River Thames

A.C. HENDERSON F.S.A. 1938

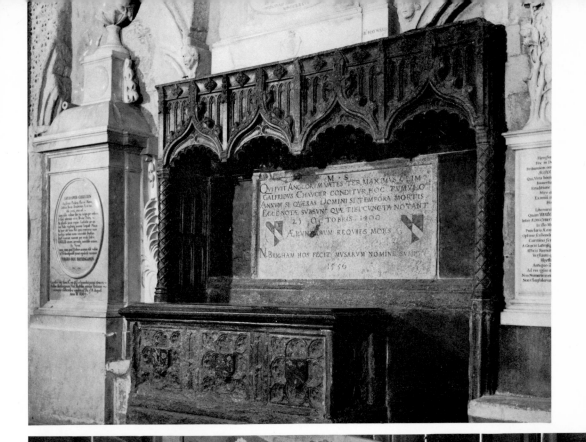

The Western Towers built between 1732 and
1745 to the design of Hawksmoor now form
the most famous view of the Abbey.

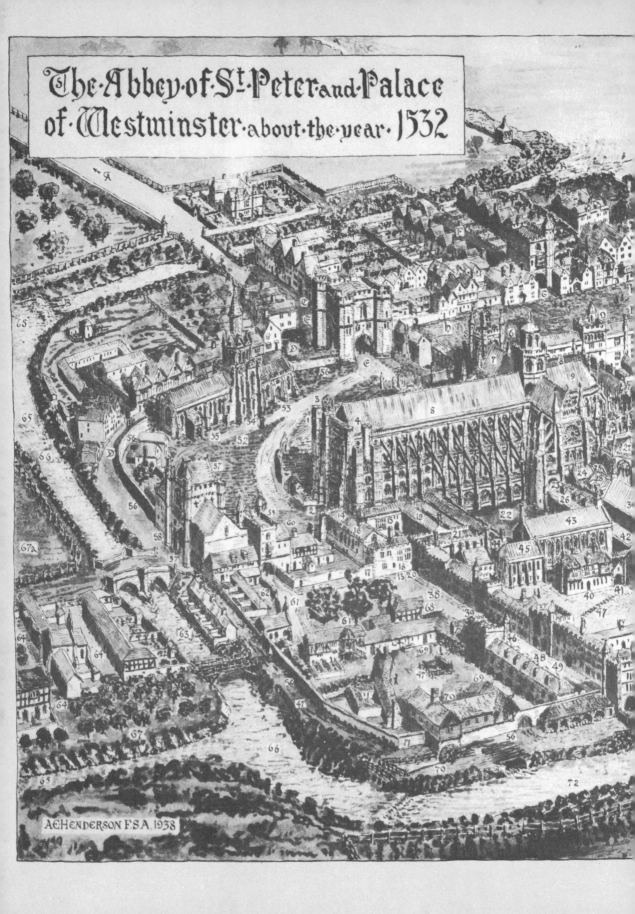

The·Abbey·of·St·Peter·and·Palace
of·Westminster·about·the·year·1532

A.E.HENDERSON F.S.A. 1938